Greece and Our American Heritage

By Doraine Bennett

STATE STANDARDS PUBLISHING®

Your State • Your Standards • Your Grade Level

Dear Educators, Librarians and Parents . . .

Thank you for choosing books from State Standards Publishing! This book supports state Departments of Educations' standards for elementary level social studies and has been measured by the ATOS Readability Formula for Books (Accelerated Reader), the Lexile Framework for Reading, and the Fountas & Pinnell Benchmark Assessment System for Guided Reading. Photographs and/or illustrations, captions, and other design elements have been included to provide supportive visual messaging to enhance text comprehension. Glossary and Word Index sections introduce key new words and help young readers develop skills in locating and combining information. Things to do and think about provide parents and teachers with resources for additional learning activity. We wish you all success in using this book to meet your student or child's learning needs.

Jill Ward, President

Publisher
State Standards Publishing, LLC
1788 Quail Hollow
Hamilton, GA 31811
USA
1.866.740.3056
www.statestandardspublishing.com

Library of Congress Cataloging-in-Publication Data
Bennett, Doraine, 1953-
 Greece and our American heritage / by Doraine Bennett.
   p. cm.
 Includes index.
 ISBN-13: 978-1-935077-71-8 (hardcover)
 ISBN-10: 1-935077-71-6 (hardcover)
 ISBN-13: 978-1-935077-72-5 (pbk.)
 ISBN-10: 1-935077-72-4 (pbk.)
 1. Greece--Civilization--To 146 B.C.--Juvenile literature. 2. Civilization, Modern--Greek influences--Juvenile literature. I. Title.
 UB270.5.B466 2009
 938--dc22

                    2009026812

About the Author

Doraine Bennett has a degree in professional writing from Columbus State University in Columbus, Georgia, and has been writing and teaching writing for over twenty years. She has authored numerous articles in magazines for both children and adults, and is the editor of the National Infantry Association's *Infantry Bugler* magazine. Doraine enjoys reading and writing books and articles for children. She lives in Georgia with her husband, Cliff.

Table of Contents

A Long Time Ago in a Place Far Away

Two thousand five hundred years ago, the Greeks changed the world. They gave us a lot of our American **heritage**. Our heritage is our way of life. Look at the map. It doesn't seem possible, does it? Greece is only a small country on the Mediterranean Sea. How did they do it?

America   Greece

Greeks gave us our American heritage.

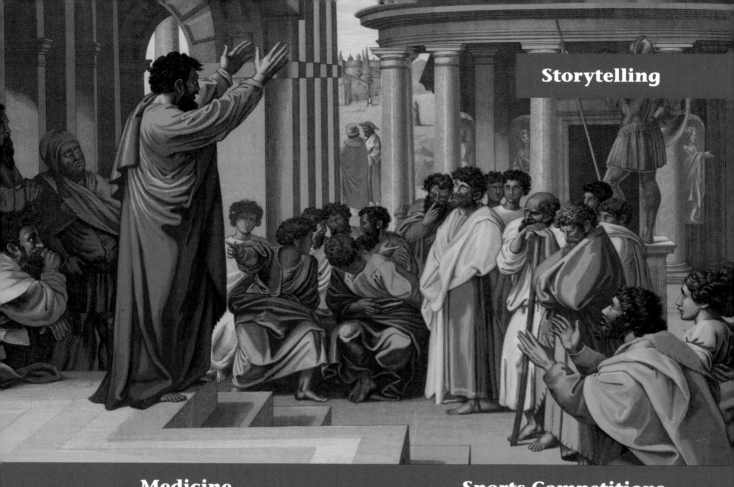

Storytelling

Medicine

Sports Competitions

6

Greeks were the first people to add vowels to the alphabet. The Greeks developed the best way to tell stories. Our stories today have a beginning, middle, and end because of the Greeks. They were the first to use medicine instead of magic for healing sickness. Greek scientists studied the planets. They discovered that the earth went around the sun. Greek artists created sculptures of people in action. The Greeks were the first to make sports competitions a national event.

Sculpture

Who's in Charge?

Long ago in Greece, each city was like a tiny country, called a **city-state**. Each city-state governed itself. Each one grew its own food. Each one had to protect itself from enemies. The city-states sometimes fought with each other. Sometimes they joined together to fight another country.

City-states protected themselves from enemies.

City-states grew their own food.

10   **Athens was the leader of the city-states.**

Athens was one of the largest city-states. It was the strongest, too. Athens became the leader of all the city-states. The government in Athens was different from any other government in the world. In most places, people who had big armies or lots of money ruled. Some people ruled because they were born into important families. No country had ever let common people be part of the government.

At least, not until Athens did.

Democracy—
How it All Started

The people of Athens believed the people who lived in their city, the **citizens**, should make their own laws. This idea was the beginning of **democracy**. The word democracy in Greek means

"the rule of the people."

This is how the **democracy in Athens** worked...

The citizens of Athens ruled themselves.

14   **Citizens made laws at the Assembly.**

Every free born male could be part of the **Assembly**. This group voted on laws. They decided when to go to war and when to make peace.

Athens was a big place. Thousands of people might be at the Assembly. Any citizen could suggest new laws or changes to old ones. Every citizen could say what he thought. Can you imagine what it must have been like?

The Greeks weren't perfect. Women and slaves could not **vote**. They couldn't choose which laws to make. They couldn't become citizens.

A council of 500 citizens helped decide what the Assembly would discuss. Members were chosen based on where they lived, not how important they were. They cast lots to see who would be picked. Casting lots was like drawing straws to make a decision. Members of the council could only serve for two years during their lifetimes. They did not want one man to become powerful enough to take over the government.

Each year, the Assembly would **elect** ten generals to be their leaders. They would choose the generals by voting. The generals were in charge of the military. They also helped to make decisions about the government. Generals could be elected over and over again.

Generals led the Assembly.

18   The Parthenon was built with columns.

Temples for their Gods

The Greeks did not live in palaces or mansions. They wanted everyone to enjoy their buildings and sculptures. They were the first people to build **columns** that could hold the weight of huge, stone roofs. The government collected taxes to pay for the buildings. A **tax** is money people pay to support the government.

They built the **Parthenon** and other grand temples to honor their gods. The Parthenon was a temple built to honor the Greek goddess, Athena. It sat on the **Acropolis**, a flat-topped rock outside the city of Athens. The Parthenon was destroyed during a war. It is still one of the most famous buildings in the world.

What Happened to Them?

The Greek world didn't remain strong. Wars came. The Greeks were conquered.

Years later in the 1700s, people remembered what the ancient Greeks had done. Artists wanted to design sculptures like the Greeks. Teachers wanted to learn about Greek history. Scientists wanted to understand Greek inventions. Actors wanted to perform Greek plays. People wanted to think like the Greeks.

In **America**, people were **thinking** about **independence from England.**

The Greeks were conquered.

Greek Inventions **Greek Plays** **Greek Sculpture**

21

American patriots wanted democracy.

The Constitution said the people would govern.

American Patriots and Ancient Greeks

Thomas Jefferson, John Adams, and Benjamin Franklin studied the ancient Greeks. These American patriots read about democracy in Athens. The people of America wanted to govern themselves. They didn't want the king of England to make their laws. They wrote the **Declaration of Independence**. It said that all men are created equal. It said that the people of America should decide how they would be ruled. They went to war to prove that what they believed was true.

After the war, Americans wrote the **Constitution of the United States**. The constitution explained how democracy in America would work.

Is American Democracy Different?

The Greek government was a **direct democracy**. Every citizen could come to the Assembly and vote. There were some problems with this method. An Assembly could be loud and confusing. A lot of people lived in Athens. Some men lived too far away. Some were too busy to attend.

America was a large country, too. It was much larger than Athens. Every citizen could not meet in one place to vote on laws. The American Constitution created a **representative democracy**. The people voted. They elected leaders to **represent** them. These leaders spoke for the people. The leaders made the laws.

People in America elect leaders to represent them.

Vote John Doe for Senator

26   **The U.S. Supreme Court**

The Capitol of Virginia

Building Like the Greeks

Thomas Jefferson studied **architecture**, the way things are built. He believed a building was a symbol of our American **ideals**, the things we believe. He believed that American buildings should be different from the buildings in England. He wanted public buildings to make people think about democracy. He made them look like Greek buildings.

Jefferson designed the capitol of Virginia in Richmond. It was the first building in America that looked like an ancient Greek temple. The main entrance to the U.S. Supreme Court has sixteen tall Greek columns. Today, people all over America have buildings with tall columns like the Greeks.

The Greeks Changed the World

The Greeks gave us democracy as our form of government. The Greeks gave us scientific ways to think about medicine. They helped us understand our planet and the science of **astronomy**, the study of the planets and the universe. The Greeks started the **Olympic Games**. Today, athletes from all over the world compete in the Olympics. Many of our buildings have Greek columns. They make us think about democracy.

The **ancient Greeks** really did **change** the **world**.

Democratic Government

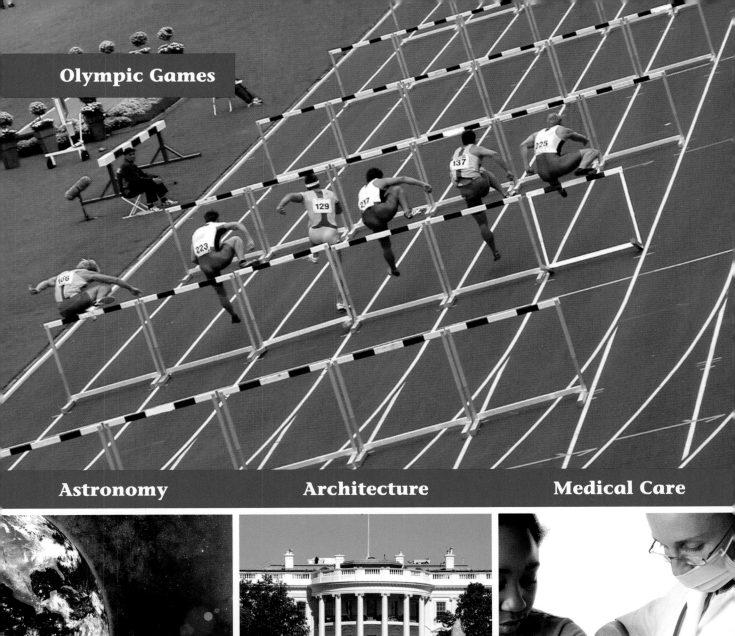

Olympic Games

Astronomy

Architecture

Medical Care

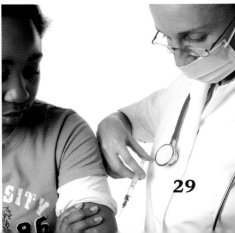

29

Glossary

Acropolis – A flat-topped rock outside Athens where the Parthenon was built.

architecture – The way things are built.

Assembly – A group of citizens in ancient Greece who voted on laws.

astronomy – The study of the planets and the universe.

Athens – The leading city-state in ancient Greece.

citizens – The people who live in a place and can make their own laws.

city-state – Cities in ancient Greece that governed themselves.

columns – Structures used by the Greeks to hold up huge stone roofs.

Constitution of the United States – A document that explained how democracy would work in America.

Declaration of Independence – A document that said Americans would be independent from England and would make their own laws.

democracy – The rule of the people.

direct democracy – The form of government in ancient Greece where every citizen voted on laws.

elect – To choose leaders by voting.

heritage – Our way of life.

ideals – The things we believe.

Olympic Games – A sports competition that started in ancient Greece.

Parthenon – A grand temple built with columns.

represent – To speak for someone else.

representative democracy – The form of government in America where the people elect leaders to represent them and make laws.

tax – Money people pay to support the government.

vote – To make decisions about laws or choose someone to represent you.

Word Index

Image Credits

Things to think about:

1. In Athens, only men were allowed to vote. When American democracy began, do you know who could vote? How has that changed?
2. Members of the council of 500 were chosen based on where they lived. How is that similar to the way members of Congress are chosen in America?
3. Members of the council could only serve for two years. Does our democracy have similar limits?
4. Compare the Greek generals and the American president. How are they the same? How are they different?
5. The Greeks collected taxes to pay for building their temples. In America, how does the government use the taxes it collects?

Things to do:

1. Find buildings in your community that have columns like the Greek temples. What kind of buildings are they?
2. Compare direct democracy and representative democracy in your class. First, decide on an issue you want to vote on. You might choose whether to have recess or watch a video. You might decide whether to eat lunch at your desks or in the cafeteria. Let everyone vote on the issue. This is the way a direct democracy works.

    Next, divide your class into groups. Let each group elect one person, a representative, from the group to vote for them. The group should tell the representative how they want him or her to vote on the issue. Then, let the representatives vote.

    Was the result the same? Why or why not?